POETRY

— TO —

HEAL YOUR BLUES

For Jenny Factor, who shared her favorites
and for Rafael Campo, who has shown how poetry can heal

POETRY
— TO —
HEAL
YOUR
BLUES

Compiled by Marilyn Hacker

MQP

Contents

Preface

What *is* "The Blues?" Originally an African-American expression for a feeling that's universal (the Brazilian-Portuguese word *saudade* is a near equivalent) but nonetheless not easy to define, it's a kind of un-ease of the spirit (one blues lyric begins "Trouble in Mind,") which may begin with a private or collective sorrow, and yet can overcome us without a specific cause for grief.

The blues may be self-generated, rise from internal discontent, but it's not the pathology called depression. And "the blues" is a kind of song as well as a state of mind: indeed, it's a state of mind we know to name because of its expression in lyrics: lyrics meant to alleviate, to heal the very unease which brought them into existence, from which they got their name.

What, then, could be more natural than to collect a group of lyrics—with the intention of both acknowledging and easing the blues? A few of the poems you'll find here touch on "the blues" as a musical form with a history—others bring different forms of music to healing. Some poems indicate other alternatives to sorrow, remedies for loss: perceptions of the seasons, animals, the natural world in all its wonder, including that distinct "nature" we make for ourselves in building great cities with all their potential for discovery.

Often the alternative is within us, when we look for it, in memory, in opening one's senses to a dawning day or the beauty of night, to the solace in friendship or solitude, to the memory or observation of childhood. Finding the words and singing the blues has always been one way to heal the blues, and this many-voiced concert is meant to brighten your own spirits.

Marilyn Hacker

The problem of gratified desire

If she puts honey in her tea
and praises prudence in the stirring up
she drinks, finally,
a drop of perfect sweetness
hot at the bottom of the cup.

There will be
pleasures more complex than it
(pleasure exchanged were infinite)
but none so cheap
more neat or definite.

Marie Ponsot

"Heaven" – is what I cannot reach!

"Heaven" – is what I cannot reach!
The Apple on the Tree
Provided it do hopeless – hang –
That – "Heaven" is – to Me!

The Color, on the Cruising Cloud –
The interdicted Land –
Behind the Hill – the House behind –
There "Heaven"– Paradise – is found!

Her teasing Purples – Afternoons –
The credulous – decoy –
Enamored – of the Conjuror –
That spurned us –Yesterday!

Emily Dickinson

Welcome joy and welcome sorrow

Welcome joy, and welcome sorrow,
  Lethe's weed and Hermes' feather;
Come today, and come tomorrow,
  I do love you both together!
  I love to mark sad faces in fair weather,
And hear a merry laugh amid the thunder.
  Fair and foul I love together:
  Meadows sweet where flames burn under,
  And a giggle at a wonder;
  Visage sage at pantomime;
  Funeral, and steeple-chime;
  Infant playing with a skull;
  Morning fair, and storm-wrecked hull;
  Nightshade with the woodbine kissing;
  Serpents in red roses hissing;
  Cleopatra regal-dressed
  With the aspics at her breast
  Dancing music, music sad,
  Both together, sane and mad;
  Muses bright and Muses pale;
  Sombre Saturn, Momus hale.
  Laugh and sigh, and laugh again –
  O the sweetness of the pain!
  Muses bright and Muses pale,
  Bare your faces of the veil!
  Let me see! and let me write
  Of the day and of the night –

Both together. Let me slake
All my thirst for sweet heart-ache!
Let my bower be of yew,
Interwreathed with myrtles new,
Pines and lime-trees full in bloom,
And my couch a low grass tomb.

John Keats

Crossroads

Crossed over the river and the river went dry
Crossed over the river, the river went dry
Saw myself drowning and I couldn't see why

Come up for air and the day said noon
Come up for air, said the air read noon
Day said, Son, you better mind something soon

Sink back down, felt my spirits leave high
Sink back down, I felt my spirits lift high
Didn't know if I was gonna die

A man give his hand and he pulled me to the shore
Man give his hand, pulled me over to the shore
Told me if I come I wouldn't drown no more

Me and the man walked and talked all day and night
Me and the man, we walked, we talked all day and night
We started wrestling til the very lip of light

I put my mind on evil sitting in my soul
Put my mind on evil just a-sitting on my soul
Struggling with the devil make a soul old

I looked at my face and my life seem small
Looked hard at my face and this life it look so small
All of a sudden didn't bother me at all

Returned to the river and I stood at the shore
Went back to the river and I stood right at the shore
Decided to myself needn't fight no more

Forrest Hamer

The song of Wandering Aengus

I went out to the hazel wood,
Because a fire was in my head,
And cut and peeled a hazel wand,
And hooked a berry to a thread;
And when white moths were on the wing,
And moth-like stars were flickering out,
I dropped the berry in a stream
And caught a little silver trout.

When I had laid it on the floor
I went to blow the fire a-flame,
But something rustled on the floor,
And someone called me by my name:
It had become a glimmering girl
With apple blossoms in her hair
Who called me by my name and ran
And faded through the brightening air.

Though I am old with wandering
Through hollow lands and hilly lands,
I will find out where she has gone,
And kiss her lips and take her hands;
And walk among long dappled grass,
And pluck till time and time are done,
The silver apples of the moon,
The golden apples of the sun.

William Butler Yeats

i thank You God

i thank You God for most this amazing
day; for the leaping greenly spirits of trees
and a blue true dream of sky; and for everything
which is natural which is infinite which is yes

(i who have died am alive again today,
and this is the sun's birthday; this is the birth
day of life and of love and wings: and of the gay
great happening illimitably earth)

how should tasting touching hearing seeing
breathing any – lifted from the no
of all nothing – human merely being
doubt unimaginable You?

(now the ears of my ears awake and
now the eyes of my eyes are opened)

e. e. cummings

Warning to children

Children, if you dare to think
Of the greatness, rareness, muchness,
Fewness of this precious only
Endless world in which you say
You live, you think of things like this:
Blocks of slate enclosing dappled
Red and green, enclosing tawny
Yellow nets, enclosing white
And black acres of dominoes,
Where a neat brown paper parcel
Tempts you to untie the string.
In the parcel, a small island,
On the island, a large tree,
On the tree, a husky fruit.
Strip the husk and peel the rind off:
In the kernel, you will see
Blocks of slate enclosing dappled
Red and green, enclosing tawny
Yellow nets, enclosing white
And black acres of dominoes,
Where the same brown paper parcel –
Children, leave the string alone!
For who dares undo the parcel
Finds himself at once inside it,
On the island, in the fruit,
Blocks of slate about his head,
Finds himself enclosed by dappled

Green and red, enclosing tawny
Yellow nets, enclosing white
And black acres of dominoes,
With the same brown paper parcel
Still unopened on his knee.
And, if he then should dare to think
Of the fewness, muchness, rareness
Greatness of this endless only
Precious world in which he says
He lives – he then unties the string.

Robert Graves

What the body told

Not long ago, I studied medicine.
It was terrible, what the body told.
I'd look inside another person's mouth,
And see the desolation of the world.
I'd see his genitals and think of sin.

Because my body speaks the stranger's language,
I've never understood those nods and stares.
My parents held me in their arms, and still
I think I've disappointed them; they care,
They stare and nod, they make their pilgrimage

To somewhere distant in my heart, they cry.
I look inside their other-person's mouths
And see the sleek interior of souls.
It's warm and red in there—like love, with teeth.
I've studied medicine until I cried

All night. Through certain books, a truth unfolds.
Anatomy and physiology,
The tiny sensing organs of the tongue—
Each nameless cell contributing its needs.
It was fabulous, what the body told.

Rafael Campo

In praise of feeling bad about yourself

The buzzard never says it is to blame.
The panther wouldn't know what scruples mean.
When the piranha strikes, it feels no shame.
If snakes had hands, they'd claim their hands were clean.

A jackal doesn't understand remorse.
Lions and lice don't waver in their course.
Why should they, when they know they're right?

Though hearts of killer whales may weight a ton,
in every other way they're light.

On this third planet of the sun
among the signs of bestiality
a clear conscience is Number One.

Wislawa Szymborska
*(Translated from the Polish by Stanislaw Baranczak
and Clare Cavanagh)*

Nocturne

After a friend has gone I like the feel of it:
The house at night. Everyone asleep.
The way it draws in like atmosphere or evening.

One o'clock. A floral teapot and a raisin scone.
A tray waits to be taken down.
The landing light is off. The clock strikes. The cat

comes into his own, mysterious on the stairs,
a black ambivalence around the legs of button-back
chairs, an insinuation to be set beside

the red spoon and the salt-glazed cup,
the saucer with the thick spill of tea
which scalds off easily under the tap. Time

is a tick, a purr, a droop. The spider
on the dining-room window has fallen asleep
among complexities as I will once

the doors are bolted and the keys tested
and the switch turned up of the kitchen light
which made outside in the back garden

an electric room – a domestication
of closed daisies, an architecture
instant and improbable.

Eavan Boland

Where blind sorrow is taught to see

Rain shines black where the red-and-white-light-laced
street divides and becomes two The walkers
hunch coats over their heads but no rain falls
here Through the wall between us comes your voice
you who give me shelter for the night
Foot to piston to axle to tire
to street with rain between makes music
surge and ebb with each change of light This
song finds your window across our bridge
you who give me shelter for the night
When does a bridge connect and when
divide When the wind pushes further in
to this room the sill glistens Chimes ring but
softly Your laugh rises and hushes them
you who give me shelter for the night
Sirens slur their frantic words but here
there is no danger The buttons on my shirt
have all day held in my loneliness
I unfasten them invisible
to you who give me shelter for the night
The light on the page falls just outside
the window The sheets are cool and dry
The street slicks and chills split in two Your warm
arpeggios sound through the lath and plaster
you who give me shelter for the night

Suzanne Gardinier

Try to praise the mutilated world

Try to praise the mutilated world.
Remember June's long days,
and wild strawberries, drops of rosé wine.
The nettles that methodically overgrow
the abandoned homesteads of exiles.
You must praise the mutilated world.
You watched the stylish yachts and ships;
one of them had a long trip ahead of it,
while salty oblivion awaited others.
You've seen the refugees going nowhere,
you've heard the executioners sing joyfully.
You should praise the mutilated world.
Remember the moments when we were together
in a white room and the curtain fluttered.
Return in thought to the concert where music flared.
You gathered acorns in the park in autumn
and leaves eddied over the earth's scars.
Praise the mutilated world
and the gray feather a thrush lost,
and the gentle light that strays and vanishes
and returns.

Adam Zagajewski
(Translated from the Polish by Clare Cavanagh)

Sonnet

Caught – the bubble
in the spirit-level,
a creature divided:
and the compass needle
wobbling and wavering,
undecided.
Freed – the broken
thermometer's mercury
running away:
and the rainbow-bird
from the narrow bevel
of the empty mirror
flying wherever
it feels like, gay!

Elizabeth Bishop

I wandered lonely as a cloud

I wandered lonely as a cloud
That floats on high o'er vales and hills,
When all at once, I saw a crows,
A host of golden daffodils;
Beside the lake, beneath the trees,
Fluttering and dancing in the breeze.

Continuous as the stars that shine
And twinkle on the milky way,
They stretched in never-ending line
Along the margin of a bay:
Ten thousand saw I at a glance,
Tossing their heads in sprightly dance.

The waves beside them danced, but they
Outdid the sparkling waves in glee;
A poet could not but be gay
In such a jocund company;
I gazed – and gazed – but little thought
What wealth the show to me had brought:

For oft, when on my couch I lie
In vacant or in pensive mood,
They flash upon that inner eye
Which is the bliss of solitude;
And then my heart with pleasure fills
And dances with the daffodils.

William Wordsworth

Shu Swamp, Spring

Young skunk
cabbages all over
the swamp.

Brownish purple
yellow-specked
short tusks,

they thicken,
twirl and point
like thumbs.

Thumbs of old
gloves, the nails
poked through

and curled.
By Easter, fingers
will have flipped out

fat and green.
Old gloves, brown
underground,

the seams split.
The nails
have been growing.

May Swenson

in Just-

in Just-
spring   when the world is mud-
luscious the little
lame balloonman

whistles   far   and wee

and eddieandbill come
running from marbles and
piracies and it's
spring

when the world is puddle-wonderful

the queer
old balloonman whistles
far   and   wee
and bettyandisbel come dancing

from hop-scotch and jump-rope and

it's
spring
and
      the

          goat-footed

balloonMan   whistles
far
and
wee

e. e. cummings

Hourglass

"Flawless" is the word, no doubt, for this third of May
that has landed on the grounds of Mayfair,
the Retirement Community par excellence.

Right behind the wheels of the mower, grass
explodes again, the bare trees most tenderly
push out their chartreuse tips.

Bottle bees are back. Feckless, reckless,
stingless, they probably have a function.
Above the cardinal, scarlet on the rim

of the birdbath, twinning himself,
they hover, cruise the flowers, mate.
The tiny water catches the sky.

On the circular inner road, the lady
untangles the poodle's leash from her cane.
He is wild to chase the splendid smells.

The small man with the small smile
rapidly steering his Amigo,
bowls past. She would wave, but can't.

All around, birds and sexual flowers
are intent on color, flight, fragrance.
The gardener sweeps his sweaty face

with a khaki sleeve. His tulips are shined
black at their centers. They have come along nicely.
He is young and will be gone before dark.

The man in the Amigo has in mind a May
a mirror of this, but unobtainable
as the touch of the woman in that glass.

The sun's force chills him. But the lady
with the curly poodle could melt her cane
in the very heat of her precious pleasure.

She perfectly understands the calendar
and the sun's passage. But she grips the leash
and leans on the air that is hers and here.

Josephine Jacobsen

The voice of summer

The black fig tree, the juice
Of warm fruit,
The bruised peaches,
The first sour grape clusters.

O lovely summer.

In the kitchen,
The monotonous complaint of trapped flies.

Where does the eternal soul reside?

Against the sturdy wall.
In the creamy freshness
Of kitchens,
The refrigerator
Sings with its voice full of hail.

Philippe Delaveau
(Translated from the French by Ellen Hinsey)

Poppies on the wheat

Along Ancona's hills the shimmering heat,
A tropic tide of air with ebb and flow
Bathes all the fields of wheat until they glow
Like flashing seas of green, which toss and beat
Around the vines. The poppies lithe and fleet
Seem running, fiery torchmen, to and fro
To mark the shore.
               The farmer does not know
That they are there. He walks with heavy feet,
Counting the bread and wine by autumn's gain,
But I, – I smile to think that days remain
Perhaps to me in which, though bread be sweet
No more, and red wine warm my blood in vain,
I shall be glad remembering how the fleet,
Lithe poppies ran like torchmen with the wheat.

Helen Hunt Jackson

Oppositions

Today I was caught alone in a summer storm
counting heartbeats from flash to flash of thunder.

From a small plane once I looked down a cliff of cloud.
Like God to Moses, it exploded into instructions.

Home, a yellow frog on the shower-pipe
startled my hand and watched me as I watch lightning.

Frog, my towel is wet, my hair dripping,
but you don't for such reasons take me to be a refuge.

Small damp peaceful sage with a loony grin,
('one minute of sitting, one inch of Buddha')*

a long time back, we clambered up the shore
and learned to play with fire. Now there's no stopping us.

Back to the drainpipe, frog, don't follow me.
I'm off to dry my hair by the radiator.

I can't believe that wine's warm solaces
don't help the searcher: the poet on the wineshop floor

was given his revelations. The hermit of Cold Mountain
laughs as loudly perhaps – I choose fire, not snow.

Judith Wright

Manzan (1635-1714)

Autumn

I want to mention
summer ending
without meaning the death
of somebody loved

or even the death
of the trees.
Today in the market
I heard a mother say

Look at the pumpkins,
it's finally autumn!
And the child didn't think
of the death of her mother

which is due before her own
but tasted the sound
of the words on her clumsy tongue:
pumpkin; autumn.

Let the eye enlarge
with all it beholds.
I want to celebrate
color, how one red leaf

flickers like a match
held to a dry branch,
and the whole world goes up
in orange and gold.

Linda Pastan

'O wild West Wind...'

O wild West Wind, thou breath of Autumn's being,
Thou, from whose unseen presence the leaves dead
Are driven, like ghosts from an enchanter fleeing,

Yellow, and black, and pale, and hectic red,
Pestilence-stricken multitudes: O thou,
Who chariotest to their dark wintry bed

The wingéd seeds, where they lie cold and low,
Each like a corpse within its grave, until
Thine azure sister of the Spring shall blow

Her clarion o'er the dreaming earth, and fill
(Driving sweet buds like flocks to feed in air)
With living hues and odors plain and hill:

Wild Spirit, which art moving everywhere;
Destroyer and preserver; hear, oh hear!

Percy Bysshe Shelley

Wind's split octaves

explain why I hear my heart
in the tree's leaves – poplar's water shiver,
large-palmed maples, iron-spun brown oak.

Sometimes the wind reaches so far inside,
leaving nothing unturned, I find myself
welcoming an intimate chat with my stray selfishness.
Acting as if, a ventriloquist, I feel my mouth open and
    close
just to let the air sweep in
and out comes a giddy howl of laughter
stirring blood to my cheeks.
Arrow leaf falls
sharp, angry among the others
and wind comes, covers the ground,
sends up loneliness
helpless against itself –
wind leaves love
among the ruined.

Sun passes into tree,
copper sheath, birch bark white
grows a house within a house
roof of shining leaves.

Beatrix Gates

The egg

The old woman wipes an egg
with her work apron
a heavy egg the color of ivory
that no one else can claim
then she looks at the autumn
through the skylight
and it's like a delicate picture
confined to a single image
there is nothing
out of season
and the fragile egg
she holds in her palm
is the one new thing.

Jean Follain
(Translated from the French by Stephen Romer)

Snow

The room was suddenly rich and the great bay-window was
Spawning snow and pink roses against it
Soundlessly collateral and incompatible:
World is suddener than we fancy it.

World is crazier and more of it than we think,
Incorrigibly plural. I peel and portion
A tangerine and spit the pips and feel
The drunkenness of things being various.

And the fire flames with a bubbling sound for world
Is more spiteful and gay than one supposes –
On the tongue on the eyes on the ears in the palms of one's
      hands –
There is more than glass between the snow and the huge
      roses.

Louis Macneice

Listen

I threw a snowball across the backyard.
My dog ran after it to bring it back.
It broke as it fell, scattering snow over snow.
She stood confused, seeing and smelling nothing.
She searched in widening circles until I called her.

She looked at me and said as clearly in silence
as if she had spoken,
I know it's here, I'll find it,
went back to the center and started the circles again.

I called her two more times before she came
slowly, stopping once to look back.

That was this morning. I'm sure that she's forgotten.
I've had some trouble putting it out of my mind.

Miller Williams

Why they love us

Vanna, 1987?-1995

Dogs love us uncomplainingly because
They see us in a way we never do.
They don't have sense enough to see our flaws

The way we fear our lovers' fangs and claws.
Blondi loved Hitler; Checkers, Nixon too.
They love us uncomplainingly because

When swatted with the news for muddy paws
Or chewing on that Bruno Magli shoe
They don't have sense enough to see our flaws.

We live by common sense and logic's laws:
With dogs, forget it. Even if they knew
They love us uncomplainingly because

They're idiots, they wouldn't drop their jaws
And say, "Duh, you were mean to me. We're through."
They don't have sense enough to see our flaws.

Thank god for that. A big round of applause
For what can sniff your ass and *still* love you.
Dogs love us uncomplainingly because
They don't have sense enough to see our flaws.

R. S. Gwynn

Dharma

The way the dog trots out the front door
every morning
without a hat or an umbrella,
without any money
or the keys to her doghouse
never fails to fill the saucer of my heart
with milky admiration.

Who provides a finer example
of a life without encumbrance –
Thoreau in his curtainless hut
with a single plate, a single spoon?
Gandhi with his staff and his holy diapers?

Off she goes into the material world
with nothing but her brown coat
and her modest blue collar,
following only her wet nose,
the twin portals of her breathing,
followed only by the plume of her tail.

If only she did not shove the cat aside
every morning
and eat all his food
what a model of self-containment she would be,
what a paragon of earthly detachment.
If only she were not so eager
for a rub behind the ears,
so acrobatic in her welcomes.
If only I were not her god.

Billy Collins

Cat & the weather

Cat takes a look at the weather.
Snow.
Puts a paw on the sill.
His perch is piled, is a pillow.

Shape of his pad appears.
Will it dig. No.
Not like sand. Like his fur almost.

But licked, not liked.
Too cold.
Insects are flying, fainting down.
He'll try

to bat one against the pane.
They have no body and no buzz.
And now his feet are wet;
it's a puzzle.

Shakes each leg,
then shakes his skin
to get the white flies off.
Looks for his tail,

tells it to come on in
by the radiator.
World's turned queer
somehow. All white,

no smell. Well, here
inside, it's still familiar.
He'll go to sleep until
it puts itself right.

May Swenson

The tyger

Tyger! Tyger! burning bright
In the forests of the night
What immortal hand or eye
Could frame thy fearful symmetry?

In what distant deeps or skies
Burnt the fire of thine eyes?
On what wings dare he aspire?
What the hand dare seize the fire?

And what shoulder, and what art
Could twist the sinews of thy heart,
And when thy heart began to beat,
What dread hand? and what dread feet?

What the hammer? what the chain?
In what furnace was thy brain?
What the anvil? what dread grasp
Dare its deadly terrors clasp?

When the stars threw down their spears,
And water'd heaven with their tears,
Did he smile his work to see?
Did he who made the Lamb make thee?

Tyger! Tyger! burning bright
In the forests of the night,
What immortal hand or eye,
Dare frame thy fearful symmetry?

William Blake

Four a.m. in the woods

Darkness softens, a thin
tissue of mist between trees.
One by one, the day's
uncountable voices come out
like twilight fireflies, like stars.
The perceiving self sits
with his back against rough bark,
casting ten thousand questions into the future.
As shadows take shape, the curtains part
for the length of time it takes to gasp,
and behold, the purpose of his
life dawns on him.

Marilyn Nelson

Modern nature

For Marie Ponsot

Where the Hudson River's crests are lit
with sun as by luminescent toxin –
where the Park's colony of lab rats
twine like roots of a tropical plant –
over the Cathedral's disruption of nests
at the heralding angel's copper hem –
there is the city hawk's domain.

The scattered wings of pigeons mark
the territory where he preys.
He, improbable, feeds in air,
but when his form darkens the hardwood
of an apartment/warren behind glass
(rookery of couches and bookshelves)
the rabbit stands to look, and only
the teacups tremble in their saucers.

Elizabeth Grainger

The blues don't change

"Now I'll tell you about the
Blues. All Negroes like Blues.
Why? Because they was born with
the Blues. And now everybody
have the Blues. Sometimes they don't
know what it is."
Leadbelly

And I was born with you, wasn't I, Blues?
Wombed with you, wounded, reared and forwarded
from address to address, stamped, stomped
and returned to sender by nobody else but you,
Blue Rider, writing me off every chance you
get, you mean old grudgeful-hearted, table-
turning demon you, you soul-sucking gem,

Blue diamond in the rough, you are forever.
You can't be outfoxed don't care how they cut
and smuggle and shine on you, you're like a
shadow, too dumb and stubborn and necessary
to let them turn you into what you ain't
with color or theory or powder or paint.

That's how you can stay in style without sticking
and not getting stuck. You know how to sting
where I can't scratch, and you move from frying
pan to skillet the same way you move people
to go to wiggling their bodies, juggling their
limbs, loosening that goose, upping their voices,
opening their pores, rolling their hips and lips.

They can shake their bodies but they can't shake you.

Al Young

Alba

It's dawn again and once again it's dawn
And it's dawn again, drawn bow toward which the target
Tightens, eye forgetting its darkroom
Theater where lines colors textures reinvent
Under the sun's direction, deceptively distant,
Unfailingly for a while, how long, this stage-set

It's dawn again and once again it's dawn
With the laughter of oriole angels
Who prick their fingers mocking their sister's
Pagan veils and the sphere flies
In its rags of nerve and blood
With all the birds who skim the seas
And fold their wings on our masts, mauve upon mauve
Before breasting other seas. Never for long
Do the same eyes follow their exodus

It's dawn again and the grace
Of being an extra in this magic show
Played out trillions of times, trillions of trills
But hardly more than thirty thousand for humans
Whose figures bind their brains. It's
Dawn again, braille beneath fingers
Moist with sperm and it's dawn
Again and once again it's dawn

Claire Malroux
(Translated from the French by Marilyn Hacker)

I try to waken and greet
the world once again

In a pine tree
A few yards from my window sill
A brilliant blue jay is springing up and down, up and
down,
On a branch.
I laugh as I see him abandon himself
To entire delight, for he knows as well as I do
That the branch will not break.

James Wright

Ukranian

Before I go outside I daub my face
with vinegar. That is Ukranian. I put
one drop behind my knee and one on my earlobe.
I choose a bush. If there is a flower I scatter
a grain of sugar on a twig to help
the flying worms; I pick a weed; I prop
a rain-drenched tulip. There is a part of me
that lives forever. Spring after spring I sit
at my redwood table; at this point the grain is white
with age, the boards are splintered, the hole that held
a grand umbrella is bent, or twisted, nothing
could fit there. Yet I'm enchanted. I sit on the bench –
one of two – half-curved – the table itself
is round, it measures more than a yard, the end boards
are split and shattered. I have one favorite tree
and one favorite bird. I lift my cocoa. Water
is all around me. I make a pact; if the tree
lasts one more year, if it blooms next spring, if the flowers
that cover the twigs and fill the sky come back again
I'll stay here another winter, I'll plant a garden,
I'll trim my branches, I'll rake my leaves. The cardinal
who lives beside the redbud, he whose crimson
is richer than that pink, he who almost
shames the tulips, he whose carnal cry
is always loud and florid, he is my witness.

Gerald Stern

Weather central

Each evening at six-fifteen, the weatherman
turns a shoulder to us, extends his hand,
and talking softly as a groom, cautiously
smooths and strokes the massive, dappled flank
of the continent, touching the cloudy whorls
that drift like galaxies across its hide,
tracing the loops of harness with their barbs
and bells and pennants; then, with a horsefly's touch,
he brushes a mountain range and sets a shudder
running just under the skin. His bearing
is cavalier from years of success and he laughs
at the science, yet makes no sudden moves
that might startle that splendid order
or loosen the physics. One would not want to wake
the enormous Appaloosa mare of weather,
asleep in her stall on a peaceful moonlit night.

Ted Kooser

The pictures of my new day

The pictures of my new day
will now be colored, drawn,
by the tempera of first light
stored for me by a thoughtful dawn
which knew of my love for late sleeping.

Now, more than love on earth,
the untamed imaginings rooted under
my hair,
more than the sanded varnished scars
jeweled now I wear,
more than the silver life sign of survival
and the paid penance of poems,
this light.
It flared up one evening, a Sunday
towards seven.
I swear it descended a living shaft
of brightest light
lit from within by light.
And as if sighting the woman's love
of show
not content with the perfection of itself
perfect pole running from ceiling
to floor
it spawned and spiraled from itself
ribbons and banners of more light.
I have seen it.

Lorna Goodison

Gift

A day so happy.
Fog lifted early, I worked in the garden.
Hummingbirds were stopping over honeysuckle flowers.
There was no thing on earth I wanted to possess.
I knew no one worth my envying him.
Whatever evil I had suffered, I forgot.
To think that once I was the same man did not
    embarrass me.
In my body I felt no pain.
When straightening up, I saw the blue sea and sails.

Czeslaw Milosz
(Translated from the Polish by the author)

Easter-wings

Lord, who createdst man in wealth and store,
    Though foolishly he lost the same,
        Decaying more and more,
           Till he became
            Most poore:
            With   thee
          O let me rise
        As larks, harmoniously,
     And sing this day thy victories:
Then shall the fall further the flight in me.

My tender age in sorrow did beginne;
    And still with sicknesses and shame
        Thou didst so punish sinne,
           That I became
           Most thinne.
           With   thee
          Let me combine
        And feel this day thy victorie:
    For, if I imp my wing on thine,
Affliction shall advance the flight in me.

George Herbert

Nasturtium

Born in a sour waste lot
You labored up to light,
Bunching what strength you'd got
And running out of sight
Though a knot-hole at last,
To come forth into sun
As if without a past,
Done with it, re-begun.

Now street-side of the fence
You take a few green turns,
Nimble in nonchalance
Before your first flower burns.
From poverty and prison
And undernourishment
A prodigal has risen,
Self-spending, never spent.

Irregular yellow shell
And drooping spur behind...
Not rare but beautiful
– Street-handsome – as you wind
And leap, hold after hold,
A golden runaway
Still running, strewing gold
From side to side all day.

Thom Gunn

Various protestations from various people

Esther say I drink too much.
Mama say pray don't think too much.
My shrink say I feel too much,
And the cops say I steal too much;
Social Workers say I miss my Daddy too much,
That I dream of driving a Caddy too much.
White folks say I'm lazy and late too much,
Not objective – depend on fate too much.
Philosophers say I want to BE too much.
Reagan say I talk about me too much,
Singing songs 'bout being free too much.

I say – sing about me being *free* too much?
Say sing about me being *free* too much?

Etheridge Knight

To play pianissimo

Does not mean silence,
the absence of moon in the day sky
for example.

Does not mean barely to speak
the way a child's whisper
makes only warm air
on his mother's right ear.

To play pianissimo
is to carry sweet words
to the old woman in the dark last row
who cannot hear anything else
and to lay them across her lap like a shawl.

Lola Haskins

Twelve Bar Bessie

See that day, Lord, did you hear what happened then.
A nine o'clock shadow always chases the sun,
And in the thick heavy air came the Ku Klux Klan
To the tent where the Queen was about to sing her song.

They were going to pull the Blues Tent down.
Going to move the Queen out of the town.
Take her twelve bar beat and squash it into the ground.
She tried to get her Prop Boys together, and they got
    scared.

She tried to get the Prop Boys together, and they got
    scared.
She said Boys, Boys, get those men out of here.
But they ran away and left the Empress on her own.
She went over to the men who had masks over their head

With the hand on her hips she cursed and she hollered,
"I'll get the whole damn lot of you out of here now
If I have to. You're as good as dead. You just pick up those
    sheets and run. Go on."

That's what she done. Her voice was cast-iron.
You should have seen them. You should have seen them.
Those masks made out of sheets from somebody's bed.
Those masks flying over their heads. Flapping.

They was flapping like some strange bird migrating,
Some bird that smelt danger in the air, a blue song,
And flew. Out of the small mid western town.
To the sound of black hands clapping.

And the Empress saying, 'And as for you' to the ones who
    did nothing.

Jackie Kay

Magic flute

Suddenly I felt my heart
open like a hand
and thrust its way
out of my chest.

Awkward as a big flower
it hung, gulping oxygen.

It was the music
and the butter haired
Down's boy in front
clasping his parents
in his creased smile of glee.

He took his mother and father
like a small fish into the plunge
of the music and my heart
followed them on a string,

but I blushed for it, cravenly,
so it shrank back
blowing a raspberry
between my ribs as it shriveled

the great, glowing, vulgar
balloon I thought I had mislaid.

Kate Foley

Cello

Those who don't like it say it's
just a mutant violin
that's been kicked out of the chorus.
Not so.
The cello has many secrets,
but it never sobs,
just sings in its low voice.
Not everything turns into song
Though. Sometimes you catch
a murmur or a whisper:
I'm lonely,
I can't sleep.

Adam Zagajewski
(Translated from the Polish by Clare Cavanagh)

Perhaps I asked too large –

Perhaps I asked too large –
I take – no less than skies –
For Earths, grow thick as
Berries, in my native town –

My Basket holds – just – Firmaments –
Those – dangle easy – on my arm,
But smaller bundles – Cram.

Emily Dickinson

Londoner

Scarcely two hours back in the country
and I'm shopping in East Finchley High Road
in a cotton skirt, a cardigan, sandals –
or flipflops as people call them here,
where February's winter. Aren't I cold?
The neighbors in their overcoats are smiling
at my smiles and not at my bare toes:
they know me here.

                I hardly know myself,
yet. It takes me until Monday evening,
walking from the office after dark
to Westminster Bridge. It's cold, it's foggy,
the traffic's as abominable as ever,
and there across the Thames is County Hall,
that uninspired stone body, floodlit.
It makes me laugh. In fact, it makes me sing.

Fleur Adcock

Cathedral builders

They climbed on sketchy ladders towards God,
With winch and pulley hoisted hewn rock into Heaven,
Inhabited sky with hammers, defied gravity,
Deified stone, took up God's house to meet Him,

And came down to their suppers and small beer;
Every night slept, lay with their smelly wives,
Quarreled and cuffed the children, lied,
Spat, sang, were happy or unhappy,

And every day took to the ladders again;
Impeded the rights of way of another summer's
Swallows, grew grayer, shakier, became less inclined
To fix a neighbor's roof of a fine evening,

Saw naves sprout arches, clerestories soar,
Cursed the loud fancy glaziers for their luck,
Somehow escaped the plague, got rheumatism,
Decided it was time to give it up,

To leave the spire to others; stood in the crowd
Well back from the vestments at the consecration,
Envied the fat bishop his warm boots,
Cocked up a squint eye and said "I bloody did that."

John Ormond

The Negro speaks of rivers

I've known rivers:
I've known rivers ancient as the world and older than the
    flow of human blood in human veins.

My soul has grown deep like the rivers.

I bathed in the Euphrates when dawns were young.
I built my hut near the Congo and it lulled me to sleep.
I looked upon the Nile and raised the pyramids above it.
I heard the singing of the Mississippi when Abe Lincoln
    went down to New Orleans, and I've seen its muddy
    bosom turn all golden in the sunset.

I've known rivers:
Ancient, dusky rivers.

My soul has grown deep like the rivers.

Langston Hughes

Recuerdo

We were very tired, we were very merry –
We had gone back and forth all night upon the ferry.
It was bare and bright, and smelled like a stable –
But we looked into a fire, we leaned across a table,
We lay on the hill-top underneath the moon;
And the whistles kept blowing, and the dawn came soon.

We were very tired, we were very merry –
We had gone back and forth all night on the ferry;
And you ate an apple, and I ate a pear,
From a dozen of each we had bought somewhere;
And the sky went wan, and the wind came cold,
And the sun rose dripping, a bucketful of gold.

We were very tired, we were very merry,
We had gone back and forth all night on the ferry.
We hailed, "Good morrow, mother!" to a shawl-covered
    head,
And bought a morning paper, which neither of us read;
And she wept, "God bless you!" for the apples and the
    pears,
And we gave her all our money but our subway fares.

Edna St. Vincent Millay

Composed upon Westminster Bridge, September 3, 1802

Earth has not anything to show more fair:
Dull would he be of soul who could pass by
A sight so touching in its majesty;
This City doth now, like a garment, wear
The beauty of the morning, silent, bare,
Ships, towers, domes, theaters and temples lie
Open unto the fields, and to the sky;
All bright and glittering in the smokeless air.
Never did sun more beautifully steep
In his first splendor, valley, rock, or hill;
Ne'er saw I, never felt, a calm so deep!
The river glideth at his own sweet will:
Dear God! The very houses seem asleep;
And all that mighty heart is lying still!

William Wordsworth

A map of the city

I stand upon a hill and see
A luminous country under me,
Through which at two the drunk must weave;
The transient's pause, the sailor's leave.

I notice, looking down the hill,
Arms braced upon a window-sill;
And on the web of fire escapes
Move the potential, the gray shapes.

I hold the city here, complete:
And every shape defined by light
Is mine, or corresponds to mine,
Some flickering or some steady shine.

This map is ground of my delight.
Between the limits, night by night,
I watch a malady's advance,
I recognize my love of chance.

By the recurrent lights I see
Endless potentiality,
The crowded, broken and unfinished!
I would not have the risk diminished.

Thom Gunn

A description of the morning

Now hardly here and there a hackney-coach
Appearing, showed the ruddy morn's approach.
Now Betty from her master's bed had flown,
And softly stole to discompose her own;
The slip-shod prentice from his master's door
Had pared the dirt and sprinkled round the floor.
Now Moll had whirled her mop with dext'rous airs,
Prepared to scrub the entry and the stairs.
The youth with broomy stumps began to trace
The kennel-edge, where wheels had worn the place.
The small-coal man was heard with cadence deep,
Till drowned in shriller notes of chimney-sweep:
Duns at his lordship's gate begin to meet;
And brickdust Moll had screamed through half the street.
The turnkey now, his flock returning sees,
Duly let out at nights to steal for fees.
The watchful bailiffs take their silent stands,
And schoolboys lag with satchels in their hands.

Jonathan Swift

When all my five and country senses see

When all my five and country senses see,
The fingers will forget green thumbs and mark
How, through the halfmoon's vegetable eye,
Husk of young stars and handful zodiac,
Love in the frost is pared and wintered by,
The whispering ears will watch love drummed away
Down breeze and shell to a discordant beach,
And, lashed to syllables, the lynx tongue cry
That her fond wounds are melted bitterly.
My nostrils see her breath burn like a bush.

My one and noble heart has witnesses
In all love's countries, that will grope awake;
And when blind sleep drops on the spying senses,
The heart is sensual, though five eyes break.

Dylan Thomas

Rent

If you want my apartment, sleep in it
but let's have a clear understanding:
the books are still free agents.

If the rocking chair's arms surround you
they can also let you go,
they can shape the air like a body.

I don't want your rent, I want
a radiance of attention
like the candle's flame when we eat,

I mean a kind of awe
attending the spaces between us –
Not a roof but a field of stars.

Jane Cooper

The Zydeco tablet

Who stole my monkey and my one good shoe?
I'm a traveling man looking for someone
To love at night, but every day I'm blue.

I'd walk ninety-five miles for a rendezvous,
Barefoot and bleeding, my collar undone.
Who stole my monkey and my one good shoe?

I'm the moody one coming to sing for you,
Rehearsing songs on my accordion.
I'm in love at night, but every day I'm blue.

I waltzed through Crowley in an orphan's suit,
No salt for the beans in my stew full of bones.
Who stole my monkey and my one good shoe?

Cochon de lait, I'd swallow nails to look at you,
Say your name until my voice is gone.
I'm in love at night, but every day I'm blue.

Sugar, you're the morning star, the midnight moon.
Of all the ladies in the Delta you're the one
Who stole my monkey. You're one good shoe
To love at night, but every day I'm blue.

Alison Pelegrin

Oh, oh, you will be sorry

Oh, oh, you will be sorry for that word!
Give me my book and take my kiss instead.
Was it my enemy or my friend I heard?
"What a big book for such a little head!"
Come, I will show you now my newest hat,
And you may watch me purse my mouth and prink!
Oh, I shall love you still, and all of that.
I never again shall tell you what I think.
I shall be sweet and crafty, soft and sly;
You will not catch me reading any more.
I shall be called a wife to pattern by;
And some day when you knock and push the door,
Some sane day, not too bright and not too stormy,
I shall be gone, and you may whistle for me.

Edna St. Vincent Millay

The reception

Doretha wore the short blue lace last night
and William watched her drinking so she fight
with him in flying collar slim-jim orange
tie and alligator belt below the navel pants uptight

"I flirt. You hear me? Yes, I flirt.
Been on my pretty knees all week
to clean the rich white downtown dirt
the greedy garbage money reek.

I flirt. Damned right. You look at me."
But William watched her carefully
his mustache shaky she could see
him jealous "which is how he always be

at parties." Clementine and Wilhelmina
looked at trouble in the light blue lace
and held to George while Roosevelt Senior
circled by the yella high and bitterly light blue face

he liked because she worked
the crowded room like clay like molding men
from dust to muscle jerked
the arms and shoulders moving when

she moved. The Lord Almighty Seagrams bless
Doretha in her short blue dress
and Roosevelt waiting for his chance:
a true gut-funky blues to make her really dance.

June Jordan

Canal bank walk

Leafy with love-banks and the green waters of the canal
Pouring redemption for me that I do
The will of God, wallow in the habitual, the banal,
Grow with nature again, as I before grew.
The bright stick trapped, the breeze adding a third
Party to the couple kissing on an old seat,
And a bird gathering materials for the nest for the Word
Eloquently new and abandoned to its delirious beat.
O unworn world enrapture me, encapture me in a web
Of fabulous grass and eternal voices by a beech,
Feed the gaping need of my senses, give me ad lib
To pray unselfconsciously with overflowing speech
For this soul needs to be honored with a new dress woven
From green and blue things and arguments that cannot be
proven.

Patrick Kavanagh

Stanzas for a new start

Home for a long time fought with me for air,
And I pronounced it uninhabitable.
Then, in an old tradition of reversal,
I understood I'd left my future there.

I chased across the badlands of recession:
I'd make a bid for any cuckoo's nest
That sang the joys of owner-occupation.
No loan shark lacked the details of my quest.

Now it's acquired refinement. It's a passion
Long-pursued, a serious late career.
I've shelved my dreams of contract and completion.
Haste doesn't suit the eternal first-time buyer.

Home, after all, is not a simple thing.
Even indoors, there should be garden voices,
Earth-breaking rootage, brilliant mirroring,
A constant foliation of loved faces.

Doors are a must, but let them make a palace,
Let each room smile another, on and on –
The glittering, the plain, the small, the spacious,
The sacred and the haunted and the one

Hope rests her case in – windswept, cornerless.

Carol Rumens

At Navaho Monument Valley Tribal School

From the photograph by Skeet McAuley

The football field rises
to meet the mesa. Indian boys
gallop across the grass, against

the beginnings of their body.
On those Saturday afternoons,
unbroken horses gather to watch

their sons growing larger
in the small parts of the world.
Everyone is the quarterback.

There is no thin man in a big hat
writing down all the names
in two columns: winners and losers.

This is the eternal football game,
Indians versus Indians. All the Skins
in the bleachers fancydancing,

stomping red dust straight down
into nothing. Before the game is over,
the eighth-grade girls' track team

comes running, circling the field
their thin and brown legs echoing
wild horses, wild horses, wild horses.

Sherman Alexie

Of green steps and laundry

The man will put a large-headed nail,
Shiny as silver, into the green step,
Straightening winter's bias and spring
Thaw and his hammer will knock it crooked,
The bird come obtrusively to the bough above,
And it will have to be done again, and that
Will be important; and she will hang
Blue and white shirts and a patched quilt
On the laundry line that runs from the kitchen
Step to the yard telephone pole and sheets
That smell of winter's cold and the pulley
Each time the line is launched will squeak,
And that will be important; and neither
She nor the man pounding the clear air
Fixing the green step with another nail
Will be aware of the importance, twenty
Years later thought of by him
Who drove nails and saw laundry,
Who thought little of cardinals and clothespins
And now loves life, loves life.

Ralph Gustafson

Gentle reader

Late in the night when I should be asleep
under the city stars in a small room
I read a poet. A poet: not
a versifier. Not a hot-shot
ethic-monger, laying about
him; not a diary of lying
about in cruel cruel beds, crying.
A poet, dangerous and steep.

O God, it peels me, juices me like a press;
this poetry drinks me, eats me, gut and marrow
until I exist in its jester's sorrow,
until my juices feed a savage sight
that runs along the lines, bright
as beasts' eyes. The rubble splays to dust:
city, book, bed. leaving my ear's lust
saying like Molly, yes, yes, yes, O yes.

Josephine Jacobsen

'As for me, I love an older man'

As for me, I love an older man
who'd have remained a carpenter
without fulfilling the Scriptures.

From a plank
Jesus of the white hair
carves
a cross with multiple arms
with his heavy hand.

The women are marinating olives
for a birthday dinner, with lamb
that will never be the one in the Gospels.

He is sixty-six years old, he is not the Lord
but he has taken his son's son by the hand
and twice as old as his death
whispers
that from this wood he's making a perch for doves.

Marie-Claire Bancquart
(*Translated from the French by Maxianne Berger*)

Words, she says, used to be wolves

Words, she says, used to be wolves
they lined up on the mountain peaks to tell the moon
about the difficulty
    of climbing the slope
the complacency of the flocks
and the chaotic movements of migrating clouds

They placed their anger at the moon's feet when it turned
the black book of night
    went to sleep amidst the ranting of the pages which
spoke of a golden country
    where sleep drops into the wells with its load of
turbaned stars
But wolves   don't know the Orient

Vénus Khoury-Ghata
(Translated from the French by Marilyn Hacker)

Eve's unnaming

Not horses, but roan
against the blue-green bay,

not crocuses, but wings
folded over suns,

not rhododendrons, but fire that wilts
to straw in the rain.

How to tag
stone, shell, gull,

hands enfolding lamb's-ear,
a bee sucking the delphinium,

when the sea writes and revises,
breaks, pours out, recoils,

when the elm's leaves
turn silver at dawn.

To see in the dark
the south window strew flowers

on the chapel floor,
or wind peel a sand rose,

is unnamable
like joy,

like my love's grin
between a cap and a jacket.

Names are for things
we cannot own.

Grace Schulman

The moon

You can take the moon by the spoonful
or in capsules every two hours.
It's useful as a hypnotic and sedative
and besides it relieves
those who have had too much philosophy.
A piece of moon in your purse
works better than a rabbit's foot.
Helps you find a lover
or get rich without anyone knowing,
and it staves off doctors and clinics.
You can give it to children like candy
when they've not gone to sleep,
and a few drops of moon in the eyes of the old
helps them to die in peace.
Put a new leaf of moon
under your pillow
and you'll see what you want to.
Always carry a little bottle of air of the moon
to keep you from drowning.
Give the key to the moon
to prisoners and the disappointed.
For those who are sentenced to death
and for those who are sentenced to life
there is no better tonic than the moon
in precise and regular doses.

Jaime Sabines
(*Translated from the Spanish by W.S. Merwin*)

And no death

I hold the pen and all I can write
is that I have been here and now am gone.
May this sink into your thoughts
and make a person of me once again
in your person.

I have said the formula and you now
are elected to have this consciousness
of me blossom outwards and be given
to the first person you meet. It is
how eventually we shall all be linked up
with one another and no death
will be final.

David Ignatow

Connections

The tiny clusters of whitebeard heath are in flower.
Their scent has drawn to them moths from how far away?

When I look up at the stars I don't try counting,
but I know that the lights I see can pass right through me.

What mind could weave such a complicated web?
Systems analysis might make angels giggle.

A child, I buried the key of a sardine tin.
Resurrected, I thought it might unlock the universe.

Picking up shells on the beach, said Isaac Newton.
Catch a modern physicist using such a comparison.

I can smell the whitebeard heath when it's under my nose,
and that should be enough for someone who isn't a moth;

but who wants to be a mere onlooker? Every cell of me
has been pierced through by intergalactic messages,

and the cream-colored moths vibrate their woolen wings
wholly at home in the clusters of whitebeard heath.

Judith Wright

Roundstone Cove

The wind rises. The sea snarls in the fog
far from the attentive beaches of childhood –
no picnic, no striped chairs, no sand, no sun.

Here even by day cliffs obstruct the sun;
moonlight miles out mocks this abyss of fog.
I walk big-bellied, lost in motherhood,

hunched in a shell of coat, a blinkered hood.
Alone a long time, I remember sun –
poor magic effort to undo the fog.

Fog hoods me. But the hood of fog is sun.

Marie Ponsot

The Cambridge afternoon was gray

When you were born, the nurse's aide
Wore a gray uniform, and the Evelyn Nursing Home
Was full of Sisters of Mercy starched

To a religious ecstasy
Of tidiness. They brought you, struggling feebly
Inside your cotton blanket, only your eyes

Were looking as if they already knew
What thinking would be like –
Some pinch of thought was making your eyes brim

With diabolic relish, like a child
Who has been hiding crouched down in a closet
Among the woolen overcoats and stacked

Shoeboxes, while the anxious parents
Call Where are you? And suddenly the child
Bounces into the room

Pretending innocence...My hot breast
Was delighted, and ran up to you like a dog
To a younger dog it wants to make friends with,

So the scandalized aide had to pull the gray
Curtain around or bed, making a sound
Of hissing virtue, curtain rings on rod,

While your eyes were saying Where am I? I'm here!

Alicia Ostriker

Night feeding

Deeper than sleep but not so deep as death
I lay there sleeping and my magic head
remembered and forgot.   On first cry I
remembered and forgot and did believe.
I knew love and I knew evil:
woke to the burning song and the tree burning blind,
despair of our days and the calm milk-giver who
knows sleep, knows growth, the sex of fire and grass,
and the black snake with gold bones.

Black sleeps, gold burns;   on second cry I woke
fully and gave to feed and fed on feeding.
Gold seed, green pain, my wizards in the earth
walked through the house, black in the morning dark.
Shadows grew in my veins, my bright belief,
my head of dreams deeper than night and sleep.
Voices of all black animals crying to drink,
cries of all birth arose, simple as we,
found in the leaves, in clouds and dark, in dream,
deep as this hour, ready again to sleep.

Muriel Rukeyser

The childhood of language

for Chip and Iva

The tree isn't here, and I am
Not asleep. Sometimes there are
Children in the tree. Sometimes
He takes me out into the other room
Before the grown-ups have left.
Sometimes he holds me up
And I can touch the ceiling.
Tomorrow when he takes me to the park
I will say the right word,
I will say 'tree' and maybe he will untie
My shoes and let me walk upside-down
On the blue ceiling of the tree,
And all the grown-ups will have to watch
Me, the wonderful baby.

Tom Disch

Lullaby of a single mother

The light can only carve so much. The night
is a cricket-pressing darkness, a wet wool coat,
through the open screen, through the unlit rooms,

and my son, squatting, in the light's circle
shows me how he makes eight trucks go,
and then doesn't show me. His story plays itself
on the one-room stage our light's carved out:

Echoes of the stories I read him in his stories.
Echoes of the language I leave him in the night.
Echoes of the history I cannot say,

the ache of the body's want, the office day,
the papers in the clip on the unlit desk
and the tiny drama where they were left.
How language, simply language, sinks me;

how a work-day "No" or "You" can make
my chest slope, my shoes feel tight,
my clothes ill-fit. But now here he sits

in his patch of light:
I bulldoze rocks. I cut the hay.
I wash the sand. I smooth the road.
I lay the tar. I dig holes deep.

I hum my mother's world to sleep.

I smooth the road. I like to grate.
I bulldoze sand. I lay the tar.
I dump my load. I drag a rake.
I sing my mother back awake.

I sing my mother back awake.

Jenny Factor

Child on top of a greenhouse

The wind billowing out the seat of my britches,
My feet crackling splinters of glass and dried putty,
The half-grown chrysanthemums staring up like accusers,
Up through the streaked glass, flashing with sunlight.
A few white clouds all rushing eastward,
A line of elms plunging and tossing like horses,
And everyone, everyone, pointing up and shouting!

Theodore Roethke

Mother to son

Well, son, I'll tell you:
Life for me ain't been no crystal stair.
It's had tacks in it,
And splinters,
And boards torn up,
And places with no carpet on the floor –
Bare.
But all the time
I'se been a-climbin' on,
And reachin' landin's,
And turnin' corners,
And sometimes goin' in the dark
Where there ain't been no light.
So boy, don't you turn back.
Don't you set down on the steps
'Cause you finds it's kinder hard.
Don't you fall now –
For I'se still goin', honey,
I'se still climbin',
And life for me ain't been no crystal stair.

Langston Hughes

Top of the stove

And then she would lift her griddle
tool from the kindling bin, hooking one
end through a hole in the cast-iron disk
to pry it up with a turn of her wrist.

Our faces pinked over to watch coal
chunks churn and fizz. This was before
I had language to say so, the flatiron
hot all day by the kettle, fragrance

of coffee and coal smoke over
the kitchen in a mist. What did I know?
Now they've gone. Language remains.
I hear her voice like a lick of flame

to a bone-cold day. Careful, she says.
I hold my head close to see what she means.

David Baker

The hammock

When I lay my head in my mother's lap
I think how day hides the stars
the way I lay hidden once, waiting
inside my mother's singing to herself. And I remember
how she carried me on her back
between home and the kindergarten
once each morning and once each afternoon.

I don't know what my mother's thinking.

When my son lays his head in my lap, I wonder:
Do his father's kisses keep his father's worries
from becoming his? I think Dear God, and remember
there are stars we haven't heard from yet:
They have so far to arrive. Amen,
I think, and feel almost comforted.

I've no idea what my child is thinking.

Between two unknowns, I live my life.
Between my mother's hopes, older than I am
by coming before me, and my child's wishes,
older than I am
by outliving me. And what's it like?
Is it a door, and a good-bye on either side?
A window, and eternity on either side?
Yes, and a little singing between two great rests.

Li-Young Lee

Big Bessie throws her son into the street

A day of sunny face and temper.
The winter trees
Are musical.

Bright lameness from my beautiful disease
You have your destiny to chip and eat.

Be precise.
With something better than candles in the eyes.
(Candles are not enough.)

At the root of the will, a wild, inflammable stuff.

New pioneer of days and ways, be gone.
Hunt out your own or make your own alone.

Go down the street.

Gwendolyn Brooks

Grandmother gesture

My grandmother's hands come back to soothe me.
They smell of rain. They smell of the city.

They untangle my hair and smooth
my brow. There's more truth

to those hands than to all the poems
in the holy books. Her gesture is home.

The lines on her palms are maps:
she makes the whole world up –

she disappears it. It sings for her.
Its song is water, the sky is its color.

She unpicks all riddles and solves
the small mysteries. She keeps the wolves

from the door. She opens wide the door.
Summer comes spilling in with a roar.

Paula Meehan

Rubaiyat

For Telajune

Beyond the view of crossroads ringed with breath
her bed appears, the old-rose covers death
has smoothed and stilled, her fingers lie inert,
her nail-file lies beside her in its sheath.

The morning's work over, her final chore
was 'breaking up the sugar' just before
siesta, sitting crosslegged on the carpet,
her slippers lying neatly by the door.

The image of her room beyond the pane,
though lost as the winding road shifts its plane,
returns on every straight, like signatures
we trace on glass, forget and find again.

I have inherited her tools: her anvil,
her axe, her old scrolled mat, but not her skill;
and who would choose to chip at sugar-blocks
when sugar-cubes are boxed beside the till?

The scent of lilacs from the road reminds me
of my own garden: a neighboring tree
grows near the fence. At night, its clusters loom
like lantern-moons, pearly-white, unearthly.

I don't mind that the lilac's roots aren't mine.
Its boughs are, and its blooms. It curves its spine
towards my soil, and litters it with dying
stars: deadheads I gather like jasmine.

My grandmother would rise and take my arm,
then sifting through the petals in her palm
would place in mine the whitest of them all:
'Salaam, dokhtaré-mahé-man, salaam!'

'Salaam, my daughter-lovely-as-the-moon!'
Would that the world could see me, Telajune,
through your eyes! Or that I could see a world
that takes such care to tend what fades so soon.

Mimi Khalvati

cutting greens

curling them around
i hold their bodies in obscene embrace
thinking of everything but kinship.
collards and kale
strain against each strange other
away from my kissmaking hand and
the iron bedpot.
the pot is black
the cutting board is black,
my hand
and just for a minute
the greens roll black under the knife
and the kitchen twists dark on its spine
and i taste in my natural appetite
the bond of live things everywhere.

Lucille Clifton

Pineapples and pomegranates

In memory of Yehuda Amichai

To think that, as a boy of thirteen, I would grapple
with my first pineapple,
its exposed breast
setting itself as another test
of my will power, knowing in my bones
that it stood for something other than itself alone
while having absolutely no sense
of its being a worldwide symbol of munificence.
Munificence – right? Not munitions, if you understand
where I'm coming from. As if the open hand
might, for once put paid
to the hand grenade
in one corner of the planet.
I'm talking about pineapples – right? – not pomegranates.

Paul Muldoon

Arabic coffee

It was never too strong for us:
make it blacker, Papa,
thick in the bottom
tell again how years will gather
in small white cups,
how luck lives in a spot of grounds.

Leaning over the stove, he let it
boil to the top, and down again.
Two times. No sugar in his pot.
And the place where men and women
break off from one another
was not present in that room.
The hundred disappointments,
fire swallowing olive-wood beads
at the warehouse, and the dreams
tucked like pocket handkerchiefs
into each day, took their places
on the table, near the half-empty
dish of corn. And none was
more important than the others,
and all were guests. When
he carried the tray into the room,
high and balanced in his hands,
it was an offering to all of them,
stay, be seated, follow the talk
wherever it goes. The coffee was

the center of the flower.
Like clothes on a line saying
You will live long enough to wear me,
a motion of faith. There is this,
and there is more.

Naomi Shihab Nye

O taste and see

The world is
not with us enough.
O taste and see

the subway Bible poster said
meaning The Lord, meaning
if anything all that lives
to the imagination's tongue,

grief, mercy, language,
tangerine, weather, to
breathe them, bite
savor, chew, swallow, transform

into our flesh our
deaths, crossing the street, plum, quince,
living in the orchard and being
hungry, and plucking
the fruit.

Denise Levertov

Pied beauty

Glory be to God for dappled things,
For skies of couple-color as a brindled cow,
For rose-moles all in stipple upon trout that swim;
Fresh-firecoal chestnut-falls, finches' wings;
Landscape plotted and pierced, fold, fallow and plough,
And all trades, their gear and tackle and trim.
All things counter, original, spare, strange,
Whatever is fickle, freckled (who knows how?)
With swift, slow; sweet, sour; adazzle, dim.
He fathers-forth whose beauty is past change;
Praise him.

Gerard Manley Hopkins

A hymn to God the Father

Wilt thou forgive that sin where I begun,
　　Which is my sin, though it were done before?
Wilt thou forgive that sin through which I run,
　　And do run still, though still I do deplore?
　　　　When thou hast done, thou hast not done,
　　　　　　For I have more.

Wilt thou forgive that sin which I have won
　　Others to sin? and made my sin their door?
Wilt thou forgive that sin which I did shun
　　A year or two, but wallowed in, a score?
　　　　When thou hast done, thou hast not done,
　　　　　　For I have more.

I have a sin of fear, that when I have spun
　　My last thread, I shall perish on the shore;
Swear by thyself, that at my death thy son
　　Shall shine as he shines now and heretofore;
　　　　And having done that, thou hast done,
　　　　　　I fear no more.

John Donne

Ecstatic

Joy, use me like a whore.
Turn me inside out like Donne
Desired God to do with him.
Show me some muscle,

Sunlight on black stone.
Coldcock me about the head
Till I moan like a bell, low
As the one Goya could hear

Through the walls of
Quinta del Sordo.
Tie me up to the stocks those Puritans
Handled so well in Boston streets.

Don't let me down. I beg
You to use all your know-how
In one throttle. Please, good God,
Put everything into your swing.

Yusef Komunyakaa

To make a prairie

To make a prairie it takes a clover and one bee,
One clover, and a bee,
And revery.
The revery alone will do
If bees are few.

Emily Dickinson

Bees

Bees like big drops of honey,
bees carrying vines to the sun
came flying out of my youth;
these apples too are from there
                    these heavy apples,
this golden-dusty road,
these white pebbles along the stream,
my belief in folksong,
my lack of envy,
and this cloudless day,
                    this blue day
the sea hot, stripped bare, lying back,
this longing
the gleaming teeth of a full-lipped mouth,
they came out of my youth
to this Caucasian village
like big drops of honey on the feet of bees,
                    from somewhere in my forgotten youth,
                    from somewhere;
                    I never had enough of that somewhere.

Nazim Hikmet
(*Translated from the Turkish by Ruth Christie*)

Song

You're wondering if I'm lonely:
OK then, yes, I'm lonely
as a plane rides lonely and level
on its radio beam, aiming
across the Rockies
for the blue-strung aisles
of an airfield on the ocean

You want to ask, am I lonely?
Well, of course, lonely
as a woman driving across country
day after day, leaving behind
mile after mile
little towns she might have stopped
and lived and died in, lonely

If I'm lonely
it must be the loneliness
of waking first, of breathing
dawn's first cold breath on the city
of being the one awake
in a house wrapped in sleep

If I'm lonely
it's with the rowboat ice-fast on the shore
in the last red light of the year
that knows what it is, that knows it's neither
ice nor mud nor winter light
but wood, with a gift for burning.

Adrienne Rich

Brahma

If the red slayer thinks he slays
    Or if the slain think he is slain
They know not well the subtle ways
    I keep, and pass, and turn again.

Far or forget to me is near;
    Shadow and sunlight are the same'
The vanished gods to me appear;
    And one to me are shame and fame.

They reckon ill who leave me out
    When me they fly, I am the wings.
I am the doubter and the doubt,
    And I the hymn the Brahmin sings.

The strong gods pine for my abode,
    And pine in vain the sacred Seven,
But thou, meek lover of the good!
    Find me, and turn thy back on heaven.

Ralph Waldo Emerson

Tree at my window

Tree at my window, window tree,
My sash is lowered when night comes on;
But let there never be curtain drawn
Between you and me.

Vague dream-head lifted out of the ground,
And thing next most diffuse to cloud,
Not all of your light tongues talking aloud
Could be profound.

But, tree, I have seen you taken and tossed,
And if you have seen me when I slept,
You have seen me when I was taken and swept
And all but lost.

That day she put our heads together,
Fate had her imagination about her,
Your head so much concerned with outer,
Mine with inner, weather.

Robert Frost

The wild iris

At the end of my suffering
there was a door.

Hear me out: that which you call death
I remember.

Overhead, noises, branches of the pine
shifting.
Then nothing. The weak sun
flickered over the dry surface.

It is terrible to survive
as consciousness
buried in the dark earth.

Then it was over: that which you fear, being
a soul and unable
to speak, ending abruptly, the stiff earth
bending a little. And what I took to be
birds darting in low shrubs.

You who do not remember
passage from the other world
I tell you I could speak again: whatever
returns from oblivion returns
to find a voice:

from the center of my life came
a great fountain, deep blue
shadows on azure seawater.

Louise Glück

Wild geese

You do not have to be good.
You do not have to walk on your knees
for a hundred miles through the desert, repenting.
You only have to let the soft animal of your body
        love what it loves.
Tell me about despair, yours, and I will tell you mine.
Meanwhile the world goes on.
Meanwhile the sun and the clear pebbles of the rain
are moving across the landscapes,
over the prairies and the deep trees,
the mountains and the rivers.
Meanwhile the wild geese, high in the clean blue air,
are heading home again.
Whoever you are, no matter how lonely,
the world offers itself to your imagination,
calls to you like the wild geese, harsh and exciting –
over and over announcing your place
in the family of things.

Mary Oliver

'I believe with perfect faith...'

I believe with perfect faith that at this very moment
millions of human beings are standing in crossroads
and intersections, in jungles and deserts,
showing each other where to turn, where the right way is,
which direction. They explain exactly where to go,
what is the quickest way to get there, when to stop
and ask again. There, over there. The second
turnoff, not the first, and from there left or right,
near the white house, by the oak tree.
They explain with excited voices, with a wave of the hand
and a nod of the head: There, over there, not that there,
the other there,
as in some ancient rite. This too is a new religion.
I believe with perfect faith that at this very moment.

Yehuda Amichai
(*Translated from the Hebrew by Chana Bloch and
Chana Kronfeld*)

Any woman's blues

Every woman is a victim of the feel blues, too.
Soft lamp shinin
              and me alone in the night
Soft lamp is shinin
              and me alone in the night
Can't take no one beside me
              need mo'n jest some man to set me right.

I left many peoples and places
              Tryin not to be alone.
Left many a person and places
              I lived my life alone.
I need to get myself together.
              Yes, I need to make myself to home.

What's gone can be a window
              a circle in the eye of the sun.
What's gone can be a window
              a circle, well, in the eye of the sun.
Take the circle from the world, girl
              you find the light have gone.

These is old blues
              and I sing em like any woman do.
These the old blues
              and I sing em, sing em, sing em. Just like
any woman do.

My life ain't done yet.
              Naw. My song ain't through

Sherley Anne Williams

Moon-set

The dark will come, I said
soon now at moon-set.

And I looked out to see
our night-lady

so grave and magnanimous
go away

over our hill, smiling
a moment, no more, through pointed

spruces; and the dark came,
the snow turned gray.

Yet then slowly the gray
was silver, the snow-clad

spruces began to sparkle,
and even the frost of the air

was illumined, a slow
mazy

dance of light-specks. I
looked overhead

to the stars, suddenly
so present, so much a part

of the night. The night,
I said, is all grave

and all a dance and never
dark. And on my slow

snow-shoes I danced and skipped
gravely down the meadow.

Hayden Carruth

Of many worlds in this world

Just like unto a nest of boxes round
Degrees of size within each box are found,
So in this world may many worlds more be,
Thinner, and less, and less still by degree;
Although they are not subject to our sense,
A world may be no bigger than twopence.
Nature is curious, and such work may make
That our dull sense can never find, but scape.
For creatures small as atoms may be there,
If every atom a creature's figure bear.
If four atoms a world can make, then see
What several worlds might in an ear-ring be.
For millions of these atoms may be in
The head of one small, little, single pin.
And if thus small, then ladies well may wear
A world of worlds as pendants in each ear.

Margaret Cavendish, Duchess of Newcastle

Index of first lines

Biographical notes

Compiled by the publishers

Fleur Adcock (1934–): Born in New Zealand, she now lives in England. A collected edition of her poetry, *Poems 1960-2000,* was published in 2000. She also edited *The Faber Book of 20th Century Women's Poetry.*

Sherman Alexie (1966–): A Spokane/Coeur d'Alene Indian, he was born on the Spokane Indian Reservation in Wellpinit, Washington. His books of poetry include *One Stick Song* (2000), *The Summer of Black Widows* (1996), *Old Shirts & New Skins* (1993), and *The Business of Fancydancing* (1992). His novels and short fiction include *Ten Little Indians* (2003), and *The Lone Ranger and Tonto Fistfight in Heaven* (1993).

Yehuda Amichai (1924–2000): Born in Germany, emigrated to Palestine in 1936. World-famous contemporary Hebrew poet. His collections in English include *Open Closed Open* (2000), translated by Chana Bloch and Chana Kronfeld, and *Selected Poetry* (1996).

David Baker (1954–): Born in Bangor, Maine. He is Poetry Editor of *The Kenyon Review*, and currently holds the Thomas B. Fordham Chair of Creative Writing at Denison University. His books include *The Truth About Small Towns* and *Changeable Thunder.*

Marie-Claire Bancquart (1932–): Important French contemporary poet. Her recent books include *Anamorphoses* (2004) and *Rituel d'emportement* (2002). She is Professor Emerita of French literature at the Sorbonne.

Elizabeth Bishop (1911–1979): Born in Massachusetts, she grew up in Canada, and lived much of her life in Brazil. She won every major US poetry award including the Pulitzer Prize for Poetry, and the National Book Award. Her *Complete Poems* were published in 1983.

William Blake (1757–1827): Author of *Songs of Innocence* and *Songs of Experience.* Poet and engraver, now world famous for his visionary works, Blake's genius was not widely recognized in his day.

Eavan Boland (1944–): Born in Ireland. Her books include *Against Love Poetry* (2001), *The Lost Land* (1998), *In a Time of Violence* (1994), and books of prose, *Object Lessons: The Life of the Woman*, and *The Poet in Our Time* (1995).

Gwendolyn Brooks (1917–2000): Born in Kansas. In 1950 she was the first African-American poet to win the Pulitzer Prize for her book *Annie Allen*. Later books included *The Bean-Eaters* and *In the Mecca*. Her collected poems are available in the volume *Blacks*.

Rafael Campo (1964–): A Cuban-American born in New Jersey, he is an award-winning poet and practicing physician. Campo's poetry collections include *What the Body Told* and *Landscape With Human Figure*. His essay collections include *The Healing Art: A Doctor's Black Bag of Poetry*.

Hayden Carruth (1921–): Born in Connecticut, he lived for many years in Vermont and now lives in upstate New York. He is also known for his essays on contemporary poetry and on jazz. Carruth received the National Book Award for Poetry for *Scrambled Eggs and Whiskey* in 1996. His most recent collection is *Doctor Jazz* (2002).

Margaret Cavendish (1623–1673): Born into an aristocratic English family, she was Maid of Honor to Queen Henrietta Maria. Her agile imagination expressed itself in various forms, including poetry—she published her first book *Poems and Fancies* in 1653.

Lucille Clifton (1936–): Born in Depew, New York. *Blessing the Boats: New and Selected Poems*, won the National Book Award for Poetry in 2001. Other books include *The Terrible Stories* (1995), nominated for the National Book Award, *The Book of Light* (1993), *Quilting: Poems 1987–1990* (1991), *Good Woman: Poems and a Memoir 1969–1980* (1987), *Two-Headed Woman* (1980), winner of the University of Massachusetts Press Juniper Prize; and *An Ordinary Woman* (1974).

Billy Collins (1941–): Born in New York City. He is one of America's most popular poets. Collins's books include *Nine Horses* (2002), *Sailing Alone Around the Room: New and Selected Poems* (2001), *The Art of Drowning* (1995), and *Questions About Angels* (1991). A recent Poet Laureate of the United States, he was appointed New York State Poet Laureate 2004–2006.

Jane Cooper (1924–): Born in New Jersey, she taught for many years at Sarah Lawrence College. She is the author of five books of poetry including *Flashboat: Poems Collected and Reclaimed* (1999), *Green Notebook, Winter Road* (1994), and *The Weather of Six Mornings* (1969), which was the Lamont Poetry Selection of The Academy of American Poets. She was New York State Poet for 1996–1997.

e. e. cummings (1894–1962): Born in Cambridge, Massachusetts. He used experimental poetic forms and punctuation, and is admired for the playful spirit of his poetry.

Philippe Delaveau (1950–): Acclaimed French poet, he is the author of several collections of poetry—his latest is called *Instants d'éternité Faillible (Moments of Fallible Eternity)*.

Emily Dickinson (1830–1886): A giant presence in 19th-century American poetry, she lived as a virtual recluse at her home in Amherst, Massachusetts. Only seven of her poems were published in her lifetime—her work was collected and published after her death.

Tom Disch (1940–): Born in Des Moines, Iowa. Internationally famous for his science fiction novels, Disch is also a noted poet and literary critic. His books include *Yes, Let's: New and Selected Poems* (1989), a collection of essays on poetry, *The Castle of Perseverance* (2002), as well as the novels *334* and *The Genocides*.

John Donne (1572–1631): Born in London. The author of sonnets, religious poems, sermons, and essays, as well as satires, and erotic love poetry; Donne took holy orders in the Church of England in 1615.

Ralph Waldo Emerson (1803–1882): Born in Boston, Massachusetts, he was an acclaimed poet, essayist, and philosopher. He became the chief spokesman for Transcendentalism, a literary and philosophical movement that spoke against scientific rationalism.

Jenny Factor (1969–): Born in California, where she now lives. She teaches poetry at Beyond Baroque in Venice. She was the recipient of the 2000 Astraea Foundation Grant in Poetry, and won the 2001 Hayden Carruth Award for her first book, *Unraveling at the Name*.

Kate Foley (1941–): Born in London, she now lives in Amsterdam. Her books include *Soft Engineering* (1994), and *A Year Without Apricots* (1999). Foley is a trained archaeologist as well as a poet.

Jean Follain (1903–1971): French poet, born in Canisy, Normandy. He moved to Paris in 1925. His first substantial book of poems *Le Main Chaude (The Warm Hand)* was published in 1933. Collections of his work have been translated into English by Stephen Romer, Heather McHugh and W.S. Merwin.

Robert Frost (1874–1963): Born in California, he spent most of his life in New England. Frost won the Pulitzer Prize for poetry four times, and read his poem 'The Gift Outright' at President Kennedy's inauguration.

Suzanne Gardinier (1965–): Born in Massachusetts. She won the 1992 AWP Award Series in Poetry for her book *The New World*. She is also the author of a collection of essays, *A World That Can Hold All the People*. She teaches at Sarah Lawrence College in New York.

Beatrix Gates (1949–): Her third poetry book, *In the Open*, was a Lambda Literary Award finalist. As librettist, Gates received, with composer Dembska, a Meet the Composer/NEA for the opera *The Singing Bridge*. Recent poems appear in *Bloom*, and co-translations with Arenal of 'Jesus Aguado' appeared in *Poets Against The War*.

Louise Glück (1943–): Born in New York City. She is the author of seven books of poetry, including *The Seven Ages* (2001), *Meadowlands* (1996), *The Wild Iris* (1992), which received the Pulitzer Prize, and *The Triumph of Achilles* (1985), which received the National Book Critics Circle Award. She was Poet Laureate of the United States in 2003–2004.

Lorna Goodison (1947–): One of the best-known Caribbean poets, she received the Commonwealth Poetry Prize for North and South America in 1986. She now teaches creative writing at the University of Michigan.

Elizabeth Grainger (1974–): Born in Oakland, California, in 1974. Her work has appeared in various poetry journals. She currently lives in New York City, and works at Columbia Law School.

Robert Graves (1895–1985): British poet, novelist, and essayist, he survived the Battle of the Somme in 1916, and eventually left England to live in Mallorca. His book, *The White Goddess,* influenced generations of writers.

Thom Gunn (1929–2004): Born in England, he settled in San Francisco in 1960. Gunn taught at the University of California, Berkeley, as a Senior Lecturer in English. He published over 30 books of poetry, including *The Man With Night Sweats*, which chronicled the effect of AIDS on his community, and *Boss Cupid*.

Ralph Gustafson (1909–1995): Canadian poet, writer, and critic, he published more than 30 books of poems between 1935 and 1995, including his *Collected Poems* in 1987, and *Tracks in the Snow* in 1994.

R. S. Gwynn (1948–): Born in North Carolina. He is a Professor at Lamar University, and a frequent contributor to the *Sewanee Review* and *Hudson Review.* He lives in Beaumont, Texas. His selected poems, *No Word of Farewell,* was published in 2001.

Forrest Hamer (1956–): Born in Goldsboro, North Carolina. African-American poet, psychologist, candidate psychoanalyst, and a lecturer in psychology at the University of California, Berkeley. His first book, *Call and Response,* was published in 1998.

Lola Haskins (1943–): Lola Haskins's poetry has appeared in *London Review of Books*, *London Magazine*, and *The Atlantic Monthly.* Her collections include *Desire Lines* (2004), *The Rim Benders (*2001), *Forty-Four Ambitions for the Piano* (1990), and *Extranjera* (1989).

George Herbert (1593–1633): Eminent poet-priest, born in Wales. Educated at Trinity College, Cambridge, he was a member of Parliament, and was canon of Lincoln Cathedral. He wrote in English and Latin.

Nazim Hikmet (1902–1963): Born in Salonika, he is now regarded as the foremost modern Turkish poet, and has been translated into more than 50 languages. One collection of his work in English is *Beyond the Walls,* translated by Ruth Christie, Richard McKane and Talât Sait Halman.

Gerard Manley Hopkins (1844–1889): Born in Stratford, London. A Jesuit priest and poet, little of his poetry was published during his lifetime. He is now regarded as a major British poet.

Langston Hughes (1902–1967): Born in Joplin, Missouri. Poet, essayist, and writer of autobiography, fiction, and drama, Hughes was a prominent figure of the Harlem Renaissance. He published ten books of poetry, including *Montage of a Dream Deferred*.

David Ignatow (1914–1997): Born in New York City. He published seventeen books—*At My Ease: Uncollected Poems of the Fifties and Sixties* (1998), his last book, was published posthumously. He was editor of various literary journals, and served as poet-in-residence and professor at a number of colleges and universities throughout the United States.

Helen Hunt Jackson (1830–1885): Born in Amherst, Massachusetts. She was a lifelong friend of the poet Emily Dickinson, and became one of the most successful writers of her day.

Josephine Jacobsen (1908–2003): Born in Cobourg, Ontario. A highly regarded poet, short story writer, and critic, she served as Poetry Consultant to the Library of Congress (the post now called Poet Laureate) from 1971 to 1973. Her books of poems include *In the Crevice of Time: New and Collected Poems* (1995), and *The Chinese Insomniacs: New Poems* (1981).

June Jordan (1936–2002): Born in New York City's Harlem. Jordan founded the community group Poetry for the People in Berkeley California, where she taught. Her many collections of poems include *Kissing God Goodbye* (1997), *Haruko/Love Poems* (1994), and *Naming Our Destiny* (1989). Her essays include *Technical Difficulties* (1994), and *Affirmative Acts: Political Essays* (1998). Her memoir, *Soldier: A Poet's Childhood*, appeared in 2000.

Patrick Kavanagh (1904–1967): Born in County Monaghan, Ireland, he struggled to live as a farmer for the first half of his life. He became active in the literary scene of Dublin in the 1930s, writing features and reviews. His best-known poem *The Great Hunger* (1942) describes the Irish farmer's daily poverty and deprivations.

Jackie Kay (1961–): Born in Edinburgh, she now lives in Manchester. She is both a poet and a novelist. Her first poetry collection, *The Adoption Papers*, was based on her childhood experience as a black child adopted by a white family.

John Keats (1795–1821): Born in London. He died when he was 25, and had published only fifty-four poems. He is considered to be one of the finest poets of all time, and is particularly admired for his sonnets and odes.

Mimi Khalvati (1944–): Born in Tehran, she grew up in England. She has worked in England and Iran, and co-founded the Theater in Exile group, as well as London's Poetry School. She is author of five poetry collections—her latest, *The Chine*, was published in 2002, and her *Selected Poems* was published in 2000.

Venus Khoury-Ghata (1937–): Born in Lebanon, Arabic is her mother-tongue, but she has lived in France since 1973, and is the author of fifteen novels and as many books of poems writen in French. Her work has been translated into English by Marilyn Hacker, most recently in the collection *She Says* (2003).

Etheridge Knight (1931–1991): Born in Corinth, Mississippi. In 1968 Knight published *Poems from Prison,* while he was in Indiana State Prison. He became a prominent member of the Black Arts Movement. Other books include *Born of a Woman: New and Selected Poems* (1980), and *The Essential Etheridge Knight* (1986).

Yusef Komunyakaa (1947–): Born in Louisiana. His experience in Vietnam led to his emergence as a writer. His books of poems include *Pleasure Dome: New & Collected Poems, 1975-1999* (2001), *Talking Dirty to the Gods* (2000); *Thieves of Paradise* (1998), and *Neon Vernacular :New & Selected Poems 1977-1989* (1994), for which he received the Pulitzer Prize and the Kingsley Tufts Poetry Award.

Ted Kooser (1939–): Born in Ames, Iowa. Current Poet Laureate of the United States, and a writer of poetry, fiction and non-fiction. He is the author of ten collections of poetry, including *Delights & Shadows* (2004), *Winter Morning Walks: One Hundred Postcards to Jim Harrison* (2000), which won the 2001 Nebraska Book Award for poetry; and *Weather Central* (1994).

Li-Young Lee (1957–): Born of Chinese parent in Jakarta, Indonesia. His family settled in the United States in 1964, and he now lives in Chicago. Li-Young is the author of poetry collections *Book of My Nights* (2001), *The City in Which I Love You* (1991), which was the 1990 Lamont Poetry Selection; and *Rose* (1986). He also wrote a memoir entitled *The Winged Seed: A Remembrance* (1995).

Denise Levertov (1923–1997): British-born but quintessentially American poet, she worked as a nurse in London during World War II. She emigrated to America in 1948. With the publication of *Here and Now* (1956), she became an important voice in the American avant-garde. During the 1960's and the Vietnam War, antiwar activism became prominent in her poetry. During this period she produced one of her most memorable works, *The Sorrow Dance* (1967). Levertov published more than 20 volumes of poetry. *This Great Unknowing: Last Poems* was published by New Directions in 1999.

Louis MacNeice (1907–1963): The Irish landscape of his childhood is a prominent aspect of his work. Educated at Oxford University, he taught Greek before working as a scriptwriter and producer for the BBC. His *Autumn Journal,* published in 1938, chronicles the arrival of World War II in England.

Claire Malroux (1935–): Born in Albi, in southwestern France. Poet and translator from the English, she has translated, amongst others, Emily Dickinson, Derek Walcott, and Emily Bronte. Her own work has been translated from the French by Marilyn Hacker, most recently in the collection *Birds and Bison* (2004).

Paula Meehan (1955–): Born in Dublin. She is a member of *Aosdána*, which honors artists who have made an outstanding contribution to the Arts in Ireland, and has been a Writer Fellow at Trinity College, Dublin. Meehan has published several books of poetry—her most recent are *Pillow Talk* (1994), and *Dharmakaya* (2000).

Edna St. Vincent Millay (1892–1950): Born in Rockland, Maine, she moved to Greenwich Village and became part of its flourishing literary community. She won the Pulitzer Prize in 1923.

Czeslaw Milosz (1911–2004): Born In Lithuania. Milosz worked for the Resistance in Nazi-occupied Warsaw. He moved to America in the sixties, to become professor of Slavic languages and literature, University of California, Berkeley. He received the Nobel Prize for Literature in 1980. He wrote almost all of his poems in Polish, although his work was banned in Poland until after he won the Nobel Prize. He translated the works of other Polish writers into English, and co-translated his own poems with poets Robert Hass and Robert Pinsky.

Paul Muldoon (1951–): Born in Northern Ireland. He is an acclaimed poet on both sides of the Atlantic. He is currently Howard G. B. Clark '21 Professor in the Humanities at Princeton University. His most recent collection is *Moy Sand and Gravel,* which was awarded the Pulitzer Prize in 2003.

Marilyn Nelson (1946–): Born in Ohio. Professor of English at the University of Connecticut; Poet Laureate of Connecticut. Her book *The Homeplace* chronicles the history of an African-American family from the Civil War to World War II. *The Fields of Praise: New and Selected Poems,* was nominated the 1997 National Book Award.

Naomi Shihab Nye (1952–): A Palestinian-American born in St Louis Missouri, she currently lives and works in San Antonio, Texas. She is the author of several books of poems, including *19 Varieties of Gazelle: Poems of the Middle East* (2002), *Fuel* (1998), *Red Suitcase* (1994), and *Hugging the Jukebox* (1982).

Mary Oliver (1935–): Born in Ohio, she now lives in Massachusetts. She is the author of many volumes of poetry, including *Why I Wake Early* (2004), *Owls and Other Fantasies: Poems and Essays* (2003), *Winter Hours: Prose, Prose Poems, and Poems* (1999), *White Pine* (1994), *New and Selected Poems* (1992), which won the National Book award; and *American Primitive* (1983), for which she won the Pulitzer Prize.

John Ormond (1923–1990): Born in Wales. *Definition of a Waterfall* (1973), established his reputation as a one of the finest Anglo-Welsh poets of his generation. *Selected Poems* was published in 1987, and *Cathedral Builders* in 1991. He is also known for the documentary films he produced for the BBC about Welsh poets and writers.

Alicia Suskin Ostriker (1937–): Born in New York. Her books of poems include *The Little Space*: *Poems Selected and New* (1998), and *The Volcano Sequence* (2004). She is also the author of *Stealing the Language,* a germinal critical study of American women's poetry, and of *The Nakedness of the Fathers,* a feminist re-vision of the Old Testament.

Linda Pastan (1932–): Born in New York City. Her books include *The Last Uncle* (2002), *Carnival Evening: New and Selected Poems 1968–1998* (1998), *An Early Afterlife* (1995), *PM/AM: New and Selected Poems* (l982), and *The Five Stages of Grief* (l978). Linda Pastan is currently living in Potomac, Maryland; she served as the Poet Laureate of Maryland 1991–1994.

Alison Pelegrin (1972–): Louisiana-born poet, winner of the 2002 Tennessee Chapbook Prize. Her most recent publications are *The Zydeco Tablets* and *Voodoo Lips*. Her poems appear in numerous journals and anthologies. She teaches at Southern Louisiana University.

Marie Ponsot (1921–): Born in New York City. She received the National Book Critics Circle Award for *The Bird Catcher* in 1998. *Springing,* her selected poems, was published in 2002. She has also translated a collection of La Fontaine's Fables entitled *Love and Folly*.

Adrienne Rich (1929–): Born in Baltimore. Widely acclaimed poet and activist for social justice and women's and minority rights, she was awarded the Academy of American Poets Wallace Stevens Award in 1997. *The Fact of a Doorframe: Selected Poems 1950–2001*, provides a wide selection of her work, along with the collection of essays *Arts of the Possible* (2001).

Theodore Roethke (1908–1963): Born in Michigan. A critically acclaimed poet, he was awarded the Pulitzer Prize for Poetry in 1954. Roethke taught at several American Universities, and was mentor to an entire generation of northwest American poets.

Muriel Rukeyser (1913–1980): Born in New York City. She was a dedicated poet and political activist, and her work focused on the inequalities of sex, race and class. The volumes, *Out of Silence,* and *A Muriel Rukeyser Reader,* provide good introductions to her work.

Carol Rumens (1944–): Born in London. Her eleven books include *Hex* (2002), and *Holding Pattern* (1999). She has also published a novel, edited two anthologies, and collaborated in translations of Russian poetry. She is currently teaching Creative Writing at the University of Wales.

Jaime Sabines (1927–1999): Mexican poet, regarded as a major writer in the Spanish language. His awards included the Chiapas Prize in 1959, and the National Letters Prize in 1983. A bilingual collection of his work *Pieces of Shadow: Selected Poems of Jaime Sabines*, with translations by W.S. Merwin and Mario Del Valle, was published in 1996.

Grace Schulman (1935–): A native New Yorker, she is Distinguished Professor of English at the City University of New York. Schulman is poetry editor of *The Nation,* and editor of a new edition of Marianne Moore's poems. Her selected poems *Days of Wonder,* was published in 2002 following *The Painting Of Our Lives* in 2001.

Percy Bysshe Shelley (1792–1822): Born in Sussex. Quintessential English Romantic poet, and friend of Lord Byron, his rebellious political views and unorthodox lifestyle led him to abandon England for Italy, where Byron was already living.

Gerald Stern (1925–): Born In Pittsburgh. He received the National Book Award for Poetry in 1998 for *This Time: New and Selected Poems.* Subsequent books include *Last Blue* (2000), and *American Sonnets* (2002). Stern was a teacher at the University of Iowa Writers' Workshop for many years

May Swenson (1913–1989): Born in Utah. Her poetry is prized for its fine observations of the natural world. She served as a Chancellor of The Academy of American Poets from 1980 to 1989. Her work is available in the collections *Nature* and *The Love Poems of May Swenson.*

Jonathan Swift (1667–1745): Born in Dublin, he was a prolific author and polemicist. A gifted poet and brilliant satirist, he is admired both for prose works, such as *Gulliver's Travels*, and for his poetry.

Wislawa Szymborska (1923–): Born in western Poland. She has lived in Kraków since 1931. Her collections available in English include, *Miracle Fair: Selected Poems of Wislawa Szymborska* (2001), translated by Joanna Trzeciak; *View with a Grain of Sand: Selected Poems* (1995), translated by Stanislaw Baranczak and Clare Cavanagh; and *People on a Bridge* (1990), translated by Adam Czerniawski. Wislawa Szymborska won the Nobel Prize for Literature in 1996.

Dylan Thomas (1914–1953): Born in Wales. Thomas moved to London and became renowned for his vivid, lyrical poetry and popular radio plays, including *Under Milk Wood*. He visited America several times to give poetry readings, and died in New York City during his last visit.

Miller Williams (1930–): Highly regarded American poet. He has held a number of important positions including Fulbright Professor of American Studies at the National University of Mexico. He read his poem 'Of History and Hope' at President Clinton's inauguration in 1997.

Sherley Anne Williams (1944–1999): Her first book of poetry, *The Peacock Poems,* was nominated for a Pulitzer Prize in 1975. Her other books include *Some One Sweet Angel Chile (poems) 1982*, and the novel *Dessa Rose* (1986).

William Wordsworth (1770–1850): Born in Cumbria, Northumberland. His preface to his *Lyrical Ballads* was a radical literary statement, and established the importance of using common language in poetry.

James Wright (1927–1980): Born in Ohio. A highly esteemed American poet who won the Pulitzer Prize for Literature in 1966. His collected poems are available in the volume *Above the River*.

Judith Wright (1915–2000): Born in New South Wales. A militant for ecology and Aboriginal rights, she was the first Australian to win the Queen's Gold Medal for Poetry. Her books include *Human Pattern Selected Poems* (1992) and *Collected Poems* (1994).

W. B. Yeats (1865–1939): Born in Dublin, he is one of the greatest Irish poets. Yeats received the Nobel Prize for Literature in 1923.

Al Young (1939–): Born in Mississippi. His volumes of poetry include *Heaven: Collected Poems, 1956–90* (1992), *The Blues Don't Change: New and Selected Poems* (1982), and *Geography of the Near Past* (1976). His memoir *Bodies and Soul: Musical Memoirs* (1981), won the American Book Award. He was also the editor of *African American Literature: A Brief Introduction and Anthology* (1995).

Adam Zagajewski (1945–): One of Poland's most noted contemporary poets, he is currently co-editor of *Zeszyty literackie* (Literary Review), which is published in Paris. *Without End,* his selected poems in English, translation by Clare Cavanagh and other translators, was published in 2002.

Sources & Acknowledgements

Fleur Adcock: 'Londoner' from *Poems 1960–2000* (Bloodaxe Books, 2000), by permission of the publisher; Sherman Alexie: 'At Navaho Monument Valley Tribal School' from *The Business of Fancydancing: Stories and Poems* (Hanging Loose Press, 1992); Yehuda Amichai: 'I Wasn't One Of The Six Million: And What Is My Life Span?' translated by Chana Bloch and Chana Kronfeld, from *Open Closed Open: Poems* (Harcourt, 2000), © 2000 by Yehuda Amichai, English translation © 2000 by Chana Bloch and Chana Kronfeld, by permission of the publisher; David Baker: 'Top of the Stove' from *The Truth About Small Towns* (University of Arkansas Press, 1994); Marie-Claire Bancquart: 'As for me, I love an older man' translated by Maxianne Berger, from *Poetry Magazine* (October–November, 2000); Elizabeth Bishop: 'Sonnet' from *The Complete Poems 1927–1979* (The Hogarth Press, 1984), © 1979, 1983 by Alice Helen Methfessel; Eavan Boland: 'Nocturne' from *The Journey & Other Stories* (Carcanet Press, 1987), by permission of the publisher; Gwendolyn Brooks: 'Big Bessie Throws Her Son Into The Street' from *Selected Poems* (Harper Perennial, 1999); Rafael Campo: 'What the Body Told' from *What the Body Told* (Duke University Press, 1996); Hayden Carruth: 'Moon-Set' from *Collected Shorter Poems* (Copper Canyon Press, 1992); Lucille Clifton: 'cutting greens' from *Good Woman: Poems and a Memoir* (BOA Editions, 1987); Billy Collins: 'Dharma' from *Sailing Alone Around the Room* (Random House, 2001), © 2001 by Billy Collins, by permission of Random House Inc; Jane Cooper: 'Rent' from *The Flashboat* (W. W. Norton, 2000); E. E. Cummings: 'I thank you God for this most amazing' and 'in Just' from *Complete Poems 1904–1962*, edited by George J. Firmage (Liveright, 1991), © 1991 by the Trustees for the E. E. Cummings Trust and George James Firmage; Philippe Delaveau: 'The Voice of Summer' translated by Ellen Hinsey, from *Poetry Magazine* (October–November, 2000); Emily Dickinson: 'Perhaps I asked too large…' '"Heaven" is what I cannot reach!' and 'To make a prairie it takes a clover and one bee' from *The Poems of Emily Dickinson,* edited by Thomas H. Johnson (Cambridge, Massachusetts: The Belknap Press of Harvard University Press), © 1951, 1955, 1979 by the President and Fellows of Harvard College; Tom Disch: 'The Childhood of Language' by permission of the author; Jenny Factor: 'Lullaby of a Single Mother' from *Unraveling At the Name* (Copper Canyon Press, 2002); Kate Foley: 'Magic Flute' from *A Year Without Apricots* (Blackwater Press, 1999); Jean Follain: 'The Egg' translated by Stephen Romer, from *20th-Century French Poems,* edited by Stephen Romer (Faber & Faber, 2002); Robert Frost: 'Tree At My Window' from *Selected Poems* (Penguin Poems, 1955);

Poems of W. B. Yeats (Macmillan, 1950), by permission of A. P. Watt Ltd on behalf of Michael B. Yeats; Al Young: 56; 'The Blues Don't Change' from *Heaven: Collected Poems 1958–1988* (Creative Arts Book, Company, 1992); Adam Zagajewski: 'Cello' and 'Try to Praise the Mutilated World' translated by Clare Cavanagh, from *Without End: New and Selected Poems* (Farrar, Straus & Giroux, 2002).

Published by MQ Publications Limited
12 The Ivories, 6–8 Northampton Street
London N1 2HY
Tel: +44 (0) 20 7359 2244
Fax:+44 (0) 20 7359 1616
email: mail@mqpublications.com
website: www.mqpublications.com

ISBN: 1 84072 861 2

10 9 8 7 6 5 4 3 2 1

Printed and bound in China

Marilyn Hacker

Marilyn Hacker is the author of twelve books of poetry
including *WinterNumbers* (1994), which won the Lenore
Marshall Poetry Prize and a Lambda Literary Award;
Selected Poems, 1965–1990 (1994), which received the
Poets' Prize; *Going Back to the River* (1990), which won a
Lambda Literary Award; and *Presentation Piece* (1974),
which was the Lamont Poetry Selection of The
Academy of American Poets and a National Book
Award winner. She has received numerous honors and
fellowships, including an Award in Literature
from the American Academy of Arts and Letters in 2004.
She teaches American literature and literary translation
at the City University of New York, and lives in
New York and Paris. Her most recent collection,
Desesperanto, was published in 2003, as was *She Says,* a
collection of translations of theFranco-Lebanese
poet Vénus Khoury-Ghata.